EMPOWERED

A JOURNAL FOR
TEEN GIRLS

EMPOWERED

A JOURNAL FOR
TEEN GIRLS

*Reflective Prompts
to Inspire
a Confident You*

CHARMAINE CHARMANT

ROCKRIDGE
PRESS

"If you are always trying to be normal, you will never know how amazing you can be."

—MAYA ANGELOU

THIS JOURNAL BELONGS TO:

_____

CONTENTS

INTRODUCTION

Welcome! You are about to embark on an exciting journey to empowerment that will boost your confidence and self-awareness. Now that you're here, I promise you won't want to leave. You're probably wondering, "How can she be so sure? She doesn't know anything about me or my life," and you'd be right. I don't know a thing about you, but I don't have to, and here's why. Confidence is like a muscle in your body. All you have to do is tap into it and train to build it up. You can think of this journal as your gym and me as your personal trainer. No matter who you are, or what you're going through, you can rest assured that this book will be a safe haven of support throughout your confidence journey.

Now, I bet you're thinking, "Who is this woman?" to which I'd say, "I thought you'd never ask!" Hi, my name is Charmaine Charmant, and I am a self-love influencer who creates content for women who want to live more confident lives.

Every day, I empower my community of more than 20,000 women from different walks of life to embrace their individuality and feel confident in their own skin, but I had to overcome my own struggles to get to where I am today.

If anyone understands how difficult it can be to feel empowered, it's me. I've dealt with my fair share of body image issues, and I struggled the most in my late teen years. It took me awhile, but one day I realized I was trying to fix something that wasn't broken. I was so lost in my thoughts that I never stopped to appreciate the abundance of what I had: a beautiful, well-functioning body that was showing up for me every day. To me, empowerment means loving yourself unconditionally. It means embracing your individuality and trusting yourself to forge your own path with confidence. It means working toward achieving your wildest dreams with no shame and doing the inner work now so that you can look back at yourself in the future with no regrets.

Self-love is a journey that is best started as early as possible. In fact, when engaging with my community, I always strive to be the voice that my younger self needed to hear, which is why *Empowered: A Journal for Teen Girls* is so special.

What Is Empowerment?

> *"A girl should be two things: who and what she wants."*
>
> —COCO CHANEL

Empowerment is about loving yourself unconditionally, embracing your individuality, and trusting yourself to forge your own path with confidence.

Popular culture makes it easy for us to feel like we're not enough. Our social media feeds are flooded with all sorts of products marketed by the latest "It Girls", making it almost impossible not to fall into the trap of comparing ourselves with others. I'm all about drawing inspiration from our favorite ladies, but losing ourselves in the process is a big no-no. We'll wake up one day and realize that we've lost the essence of who we are.

Empowered women rise above conforming to societal norms by actively listening to their inner voice. They become in tune with what happiness means to them as individuals and set the standard for their own lives. Empowerment is about trusting yourself and knowing that there is power in what makes you unique—you don't need to look like anyone else, obtain the same credentials, or live according to anyone else's standard. What works for others may not work for you and that's okay.

After a few short entries in this journal, you will begin to discover your truth. Lean into this exploration and understand that it is the key to living a fuller and more vibrant life. Individuality is beautiful, so value yours.

How to Use This Book

I want you to think of this journal as your own personal oasis—a sanctuary that will provide you with organic opportunities to increase your self-awareness on a regular basis. It is filled with prompts and affirmations to improve your mindset and build confidence. It also has a daily recurring element to get you in the habit of identifying your emotions (feel free to circle more than one emoji!), and writing down a simple one-sentence reflection. But these are just the beginning. This journal is a tool that will help you discover your *truth* so that you can step into your power and live a happier life.

In order for this to work, you have to make a commitment to connect and be present. When using this journal, it is important to let go of external expectations. Your self-love journey is not about putting on a performance or sharing what you think the outside world expects to see (like many of us do on social media). It is about being honest with yourself and speaking the truth so that you can forge your own path.

This journal will serve as a source of support for building confidence, but it is not a replacement for a therapist or medical support. If you ever feel like life is too stressful, please seek immediate help from a professional. There is absolutely no shame in prioritizing your mental health because your mindset matters.

Self-love is a lifelong adventure, and this journal will provide you with the ultimate head start. Are you ready to embark on your journey toward empowerment? A bright future awaits!

I Am Curious

Curiosity is one of the most incredible characteristics of humankind. Our interest in learning
new things and acting on them has advanced
us in ways that our prehistoric ancestors probably could never have imagined. Fundamental
elements of our existence like language, infra-
structure, and technology would not exist
without curiosity, and yet many of us actively
repress our curiosity from fear of the unknown
or what others may think of us if we go against
the grain. It's time to unlearn this negative practice, because there is great power behind a
curious mind. Cultivating your curious mind will
help you come closer to the truth of who you
are and what you want out of life.

Today I feel:

*Today I am grateful for:*_____

What does empowerment mean to you? If you had to describe your desired future state after completing this journal, what would it look like? Sometimes to get to where we want to be, we have to visualize it.

_____

_____

_____

_____

_____

_____

_____

_____

_____

_____

_____

_____

_____

_____

_____

_____

_____

Today I feel:

Today I am grateful for: _____

In your own words, can you define curiosity? In what ways do you think curiosity can add value to your life?

_____

_____

_____

_____

_____

_____

_____

_____

_____

_____

_____

_____

_____

_____

_____

_____

_____

_____

Today I feel:

Today I am grateful for: _____

When was the last time you felt curious about something? What ignited your curiosity, and how did it make you feel? Underline the emotions that you would like to feel again and write down the environments and circumstances in which you experience those emotions the most.

_____
_____
_____
_____
_____
_____
_____
_____
_____
_____
_____
_____
_____
_____
_____
_____
_____

Today I feel:

Today I am grateful for: _____

Take a moment to consider a time when you were curious about something but didn't act on it. What prevented you from learning more? What would you do differently today?

_____

_____

_____

_____

_____

_____

_____

_____

_____

_____

_____

_____

_____

_____

_____

_____

_____

_____

Today I feel:

Today I am grateful for: _____

List five things that you are curious about. Then, one at a time, write one way you can act on learning more about each of those things.

1. _____

_____

_____

2. _____

_____

_____

3. _____

_____

_____

4. _____

_____

_____

5. _____

_____

_____

"Don't let anyone rob you of your imagination, your creativity, or your curiosity. It's your place in the world; it's your life. Go on and do all you can with it, and make it the life you want to live."

—MAE JEMISON

Today I feel:

Today I am grateful for: _____

Who is the most curious person in your life? This can be someone you know personally, or any person whom you look up to. Write down qualities of their personality that stand out when approaching new situations. When you are finished, choose one quality that you admire and write a list of ways you can incorporate it into your life.

_____

_____

_____

_____

_____

_____

_____

_____

_____

_____

_____

_____

_____

_____

_____

_____

_____

MAE JEMISON

As the first African American woman to become an astronaut, Mae Jemison embodies curiosity by being a pioneer. She was born in 1956, only two years after school segregation in the United States ended, and showed an interest in the sciences from a young age. As she cultivated her appetite for learning, her interests expanded and led her to earn a degree in chemical engineering from Stanford University, as well as a medical degree from Cornell University. She went on to join the Peace Corps, where she served as a medical officer in West Africa working alongside the National Institutes of Health and Centers for Disease Control on numerous research projects. Upon returning to the Unites States, her interest in becoming an astronaut took over and she applied to the National Aeronautics and Space Administration (NASA).

Out of the 2,000 candidates who applied, only 15 were selected and Mae was one of them. In 1992, she became the first African American woman to travel to space, orbiting Earth for more than a week!

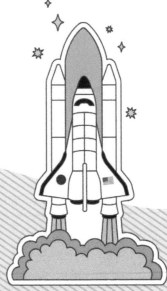

Today I feel:

Today I am grateful for: _____

Think back to a time when you tried something new. How did you feel before and after the experience? What did you learn?

_____

_____

_____

_____

_____

_____

_____

_____

_____

_____

_____

_____

_____

_____

_____

_____

_____

_____

_____

Today I feel:

Today I am grateful for: _____

How often do you allow yourself to think outside of the box? Write down 10 things that you would do differently if you knew there were no consequences, or you knew you would experience no judgment from family or friends. The sky is the limit here—go as big and extravagant as you'd like.

1. _____

2. _____

3. _____

4. _____

5. _____

6. _____

7. _____

8. _____

9. _____

10. _____

TAPPING INTO YOUR INTUITION

One of the deepest forms of wisdom comes from intuition, which is often felt from the heart. Try to listen hard to your heart. Do you hear its beats? What do they tell you? If we cultivate curiosity around our true desires, we get better at listening to ourselves, understanding the needs of others, and finding a way to achieve our goals. Feel free to write or doodle anything your heart tells you on this page.

Today I feel:

*Today I am grateful for:*_____

Think about one of your fears. Is there something about this fear that you don't understand? How can you learn more about it? Sometimes we are afraid of things that we are unfamiliar with, and curiosity can help us overcome this fear.

_____

_____

_____

_____

_____

_____

_____

_____

_____

_____

_____

_____

_____

_____

_____

_____

Today I feel:

Today I am grateful for: _____

When was the last time that you felt embarrassed for not knowing something? Reflect on that experience and write down why you felt the way that you did. How do you think things would play out if you approached a situation like this with curiosity instead of fear?

_____

_____

_____

_____

_____

_____

_____

_____

_____

_____

_____

_____

_____

_____

_____

"There is an amazing power getting to know your inner self and learning how to use it and not fight with the world. If you know what makes you happy, your personality, interests and capabilities, just use them, and everything else flows beautifully."

—JUHI CHAWLA

Today I feel:

Today I am grateful for: _____

Think about an activity or process that you do daily. How could you approach it with curiosity? Write your ideas down and consider incorporating one of them into your routine.

_____

_____

_____

_____

_____

_____

_____

_____

_____

_____

_____

_____

_____

_____

_____

_____

Today I feel:

*Today I am grateful for:*_____

Think about the last time that you disagreed with someone. What was the subject of contention? Take a moment to put yourself in their shoes and consider why they might feel the way that they did. Approaching a memory with a curious mind offers you a new perspective. What did you learn about yourself, and what would you have done differently?

_____

_____

_____

_____

_____

_____

_____

_____

_____

_____

_____

_____

_____

MALALA YOUSAFZAI

If there is one young woman who exudes genuine curiosity, it is Pakistani education-activist Malala Yousafzai. Her unwavering thirst for knowledge in the face of life-threatening adversity is what catapulted her into becoming the youngest person to receive the highly esteemed Nobel Peace Prize. Born in 1997, Malala grew up with a deep passion for learning and loved attending school in her village, but at the tender age of 11, control of her town was taken over by the Taliban, and education for young girls was banned. Unable to stand idly by, she began to speak out for the right for girls to receive an education despite the danger of defying the Taliban. Her passionate activism gained traction and was featured heavily in the media. Malala was awarded Pakistan's National Youth Peace Prize in 2011. Not long after, at the age of 15, an attempt on her life was made by the Taliban. She survived and went on to give a speech at the United Nations the very next year. She has since published a book, received numerous awards, including the Nobel Peace Prize, and founded a nonprofit organization that allows women to pursue their curiosity through education.

Today I feel:

*Today I am grateful for:*_____

Sometimes we repress our curiosity out of fear of being judged by others. When was the last time you felt judged? Write down what made you feel that way, and a few ways in which you can combat that feeling in the future.

_____

_____

_____

_____

_____

_____

_____

_____

_____

_____

_____

_____

_____

_____

_____

_____

Today I feel:

Today I am grateful for: _____

Turn your attention externally and think about the last time you judged or criticized someone. Consider why you chose that behavior. Write down ways that , in the future, you can help others feel accepted despite your differences.

_____

_____

_____

_____

_____

_____

_____

_____

_____

_____

_____

_____

_____

_____

Today I feel:

Today I am grateful for: _____

Sometimes the key to cultivating curiosity is changing your perspective. What is something that you want to overcome? What is holding you back from doing so? How can you eliminate these roadblocks or approach your obstacle from a different perspective? A little creativity can go a long way.

_____

_____

_____

_____

_____

_____

_____

_____

_____

_____

_____

_____

_____

_____

_____

_____

Today I feel:

Today I am grateful for: _____

When we feel confident, we feel more comfortable exploring new ideas and learning new things. Think about the last time you felt confident. What were you doing? What other emotions did you feel? When we start to pair confidence with actions and feelings, we begin to see patterns around what makes us feel good!

_____

_____

_____

_____

_____

_____

_____

_____

_____

_____

_____

_____

_____

_____

_____

_____

Today I feel:

*Today I am grateful for:*_____

Think about a moment when you fell short of your own expectations. If you could give yourself some advice, what would it be? Analyzing the past and being inquisitive can help us build a brighter future.

_____

_____

_____

_____

_____

_____

_____

_____

_____

_____

_____

_____

_____

_____

_____

_____

_____

Today I feel:

*Today I am grateful for:*_____

Where do you see yourself in five years? How do you plan to get there? How can you harness your creativity and curiosity to get there? You are more likely to accomplish your goals if you have a plan.

_____

_____

_____

_____

_____

_____

_____

_____

_____

_____

_____

_____

_____

_____

_____

_____

_____

_____

CURIOSITY AFFIRMATIONS

Our words hold power that we can use to improve our mindset. Do you practice speaking things into your life? Today, we will practice speaking curiosity into ours. Find a comfortable and quiet space to repeat the following affirmations:

- *"I am curious about myself."*
- *"I am constantly learning more about the world around me."*
- *"I am not afraid of the unknown."*
- *"I approach tough questions with curiosity rather than criticism or judgment."*
- *"My ability to learn is limitless."*
- *"I enjoy seeking out information about the things that excite me."*

Today I feel:

Today I am grateful for: _____

Who are two of your creative icons? Write down what qualities make them stand out. Now think about yourself. How have you been creative in the past? Are there any qualities that you share with your creative icons? Circle the qualities that you would like to embody on your empowerment journey.

_____

_____

_____

_____

_____

_____

_____

_____

_____

_____

_____

_____

_____

_____

_____

_____

_____

_____

Today I feel:

Today I am grateful for: _____

When we are happy, we are more inclined to explore our curiosity. What kinds of people, places, things, and experiences make you feel your happiest? Write them down and then brainstorm ways that you can incorporate more of those things into your day-to-day life.

_____

_____

_____

_____

_____

_____

_____

_____

_____

_____

_____

_____

_____

_____

_____

_____

"We each have one life, and we are entitled to living it on our own terms."

—FATIMA MOHAMMED

Today I feel:

*Today I am grateful for:*_____

Fear of the judgment of others can sometimes be enough to make us repress our curiosity. Are there people in your life who make you feel inadequate? Who are they? Write down a few ways in which you could reduce the amount of time you spend with them. How would that make you feel? If limiting the time that you spend with them is not an option, write them a letter explaining how their behavior makes you feel and request that they stop the behaviors that are hurtful to you.

Today I feel:

Today I am grateful for: _____

Experiencing failure can discourage us from acting on our curiosity. Think about a time when you failed. Now pretend that your best friend went through that same experience. What advice would you share with them? Is there a way that "failure" actually helped them to grow? Sometimes we are harder on ourselves than we need to be. Approaching situations from an outside perspective can oftentimes provide us with a more optimistic outlook.

_____

_____

_____

_____

_____

_____

_____

_____

_____

_____

_____

_____

_____

HELEN KELLER

Displaying curiosity in the wake of physical limitations is no easy feat, but American author and humanitarian Helen Keller never allowed her limitations to get in her way. Born in 1880, Helen lost her sight and hearing at the age of two years old. Adjusting to the limitations of her loss of the two senses was a struggle, but at the age of five, she began to learn how to read and write with the help of her teacher and lifelong companion, Anne Sullivan. Determined to learn how to speak to others, Helen attended many institutions to improve her communication skills and enroll in college. Through hard work and perseverance, she mastered several methods of communication, attended Radcliffe College, and graduated cum laude at 24 years old. She went on to write 14 books and improved the lives of many through her advocacy for the disabled, women's suffrage, labor rights, and world peace.

Today I feel:

Today I am grateful for: _____

Fear of challenging the norm, or status quo, can stunt our curiosity. Consider a practice or subject in which you blindly follow the status quo. Begin to question why that is. Sometimes expanding our mind starts with questioning what's right in front of us.

For example: *"I chose to play soccer even though I love ballet because all of my friends chose soccer, and I didn't want to feel left out."*

_____

_____

_____

_____

_____

_____

_____

_____

_____

_____

_____

Today I feel:

Today I am grateful for: _____

Reflect on your friendships. What makes your friend group diverse? What do you like about that diversity? What have you learned from having friends who are different from you? If your friend group is not diverse, consider why that is and how you can build more diverse friendships. Our differences can inspire curiosity within one another.

_____

_____

_____

_____

_____

_____

_____

_____

_____

_____

_____

_____

_____

_____

_____

Today I feel:

Today I am grateful for: _____

How can you encourage your friends and loved ones to be more curious? Write a letter to them explaining the benefits of expanding their minds and the breadth of their experiences.

_____

_____

_____

_____

_____

_____

_____

_____

_____

_____

_____

_____

_____

_____

_____

_____

I Am Resilient

The only thing standing between reality and our dreams is action. There will be moments when you will be faced with obstacles that seem impossible to overcome. I'm here to tell you that you are stronger than those obstacles. You are resilient. We all love instant gratification, but some of life's best accomplishments require preparation, patience, and multiple attempts. Do not become discouraged by hard-earned effort. Remember there is power behind your thoughts and words, including how you talk to yourself.

If we view ourselves in a positive light, our chances of reaching our goals increase exponentially. We hurt ourselves when we throw in self-doubt. It is important to remind ourselves that self-doubt is simply a mental roadblock rooted in fear—not truth. When you believe in yourself, you'll be able to overcome more than you ever thought you could.

Today I feel:

*One thing I love about myself is:*_____

Reflect on a time when you overcame an obstacle. How did you overcome it? Use that experience to develop your own resilience affirmations.

For example:

Reflection: In the middle of the semester my science grades were so low that I was afraid I would not pass the course. I came up with a plan to get extra tutoring from my teacher and was able to pass the class.

Affirmation: I can make it through anything in life because I am a resourceful planner.

_____

_____

_____

_____

_____

_____

_____

_____

_____

_____

_____

Today I feel:

*One thing I love about myself is:*_____

Nobody feels great 100 percent of the time and that's okay. As humans, it is important for us to understand that we have a wide range of emotions for a reason, and there's no shame in that. It is also equally important for us to remember that we are not defined by our emotions, as they are temporary. Reflect on a time when you felt ashamed of not feeling your best and list a few ways that you can practice grace and self-care when faced with that emotion in the future.

_____

_____

_____

_____

_____

_____

_____

_____

_____

_____

_____

_____

Today I feel:

One thing I love about myself is: _____

Our confidence is directly tied to the way that we view ourselves. Today, focus on your inner power. Think back to your three proudest moments in life and write them down. Close out your journal entry by listing three qualities you admire about yourself.

_____

_____

_____

_____

_____

_____

_____

_____

_____

_____

_____

_____

_____

_____

Today I feel:

One thing I love about myself is:_____

Failure can be a stepping stone to greatness. When was the last time that you experienced failure? What did you learn from that experience, and how can you use that lesson to help you reach a new goal?

_____

_____

_____

_____

_____

_____

_____

_____

_____

_____

_____

_____

_____

_____

_____

_____

Today I feel:

*One thing I love about myself is:*_____

Resilience requires tremendous patience. When was the last time you or someone you know exhibited patience? Reflect on the experience and brainstorm ways you can incorporate practicing patience in your day-to-day life.

_____

_____

_____

_____

_____

_____

_____

_____

_____

_____

_____

_____

_____

_____

_____

Today I feel:

*One thing I love about myself is:*_____

Reflect on a time when you exhibited resilience. What happened and how did that experience teach you more about yourself as a person?

_____

_____

_____

_____

_____

_____

_____

_____

_____

_____

_____

_____

_____

_____

_____

_____

_____

_____

OPRAH WINFREY

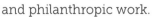

If there is one person who embodies resilience, it's Oprah Winfrey. We know her as one of the richest and most successful women in the world, but her journey was not a bed of roses. She overcame a great deal to get to where she is today.

Born into poverty in rural Mississippi, Oprah was subjected to abuse at a young age, but she did not let those experiences define her. She became a news anchor for CBS at the age of 19 and continued to pursue her passion for broadcast journalism after graduating from Tennessee State University. She eventually went on to host her own show, *The Oprah Winfrey Show*, which proved to be a huge success and aired for 25 years!

Oprah continues to touch the lives of others through her Oprah Winfrey Network and philanthropic work.

Today I feel:

One thing I love about myself is:_____

So many of us are conditioned to seek validation from others, yet the opinion that matters the most is our own. Has there been a time in your life when the opinions of others held you back? Reflect on that experience. Do their opinions still matter today? How can you prevent yourself from letting the opinions of others influence your decisions in the future?

_____

_____

_____

_____

_____

_____

_____

_____

_____

_____

_____

_____

_____

Today I feel:

One thing I love about myself is: _____

Think about compliments that you often receive and write them down. How can these accolades help you lead a more confident and resilient life?

_____

_____

_____

_____

_____

_____

_____

_____

_____

_____

_____

_____

_____

_____

_____

_____

RESILIENCE POWER POSE

Stand in front of the mirror with a straight back. Imagine there is a wire pulling you up through your spine to stand even taller. Now, place your hands on your hips. If it feels comfortable, wiggle your legs out six inches to sink into your stance. Hold the pose for five full breaths, taking in your strength and beauty. Do you feel more powerful? If you feel compelled, shout, "I am strong and beautiful!"

Modification: *You can also do this exercise sitting down. The key is to hold your power pose.*

Today I feel:

One thing I love about myself is: _____

Imagine a world in which the concept of failure does not exist. In this world, when things don't work out, we simply pick up and carry on with no negative feelings, attachments, or self-criticism. Would this reality change your goals for the future? If so, how?

_____

_____

_____

_____

_____

_____

_____

_____

_____

_____

_____

_____

_____

_____

_____

Today I feel:

*One thing I love about myself is:*_____

The more that we learn about ourselves and the world, the more resilient we can become. Experience can be life's greatest teacher. Have you ever tried something new, failed, and tried again? What experiences in your life have contributed to your capacity to learn?

_____

_____

_____

_____

_____

_____

_____

_____

_____

_____

_____

_____

_____

_____

_____

_____

"Nothing is impossible. The word itself says 'I'm possible'!"

—AUDREY HEPBURN

Today I feel:

*One thing I love about myself is:*_____

Progress originates from the belief that we have to try and fail in order to learn and grow. How have you made progress in the last month? How do you plan to make progress in the upcoming month?

_____

_____

_____

_____

_____

_____

_____

_____

_____

_____

_____

_____

_____

_____

_____

_____

Today I feel:

*One thing I love about myself is:*_____

What separates leaders from the rest is not their inherent talent, but their ability to confront failure and keep going. Reflect on a time when you kept going in the face of failure. How did that experience make you stronger?

_____

_____

_____

_____

_____

_____

_____

_____

_____

_____

_____

_____

_____

_____

SERENA WILLIAMS

World-renowned athlete Serena Williams is the epitome of resilience. She was raised in one of the most dangerous neighborhoods in Los Angeles, but her father was determined that she would not become a product of her environment. She learned how to play tennis on public courts around the city and became a professional tennis player at the tender age of 14.

Competing in a traditionally white sport, Serena faced a great deal of discrimination in the media because of the color of her skin, but that didn't stop her from honing her craft. She completely revolutionized the sport thanks to her signature style. Serena has won 23 Grand Slam singles titles, holding the number-one spot in women's singles tennis for more than six years in total!

Today I feel:

One thing I love about myself is: _____

The world is your oyster. Set a timer for 2 minutes and write down all that you want to accomplish in your lifetime. Write down as many things as you can without pausing to judge them. Remember, there are no wrong answers.

_____

_____

_____

_____

_____

_____

_____

_____

_____

_____

_____

_____

_____

_____

Today I feel:

*One thing I love about myself is:*_____

Patience is a virtue and an important skill for resiliency, but it is also a tricky skill to hone. In what types of environments do you feel most patient?

_____

_____

_____

_____

_____

_____

_____

_____

_____

_____

_____

_____

_____

_____

_____

Today I feel:

*One thing I love about myself is:*_____

Think about the last time you felt resilient. What were you doing? What other emotions did you feel? When we pair resilience with actions and feelings, we begin to see patterns emerge that make us feel powerful.

_____

_____

_____

_____

_____

_____

_____

_____

_____

_____

_____

_____

_____

_____

_____

Today I feel:

*One thing I love about myself is:*_____

You are unstoppable. Write down 10 personal attributes that make you unstoppable.

1. _____

2. _____

3. _____

4. _____

5. _____

6. _____

7. _____

8. _____

9. _____

10. _____

Today I feel:

One thing I love about myself is: _____

When we can learn to love ourselves unconditionally, we have the confidence to take control over our lives. Still, self-love is a journey. Where do you currently see yourself on your journey, and where do you hope to be in six months? What daily practices will you use to get there?

_____

_____

_____

_____

_____

_____

_____

_____

_____

_____

_____

_____

_____

_____

_____

Today I feel:

*One thing I love about myself is:*_____

Failure is not a negative thing. In fact, it can actually help us get closer to achieving our goals. Write down two ways you plan to fail in order to get closer to accomplishing your goals. Taking the pressure off of our goals can afford us more creativity and better results.

_____

_____

_____

_____

_____

_____

_____

_____

_____

_____

_____

_____

_____

_____

RESILIENCE AFFIRMATIONS

In today's exercise, you will practice speaking positivity into your life. Here are some affirmations to help you activate your resilience when faced with obstacles. Repeat them out loud.

- *"I have a lot to be thankful for."*
- *"I have a lot to offer the world."*
- *"I am proud of the work I do to reach my goals."*
- *"I have more than enough to do the things I want to do."*
- *"Fear is a normal feeling that I can use to fuel my success."*
- *"I have nothing to lose and everything to gain by believing in myself."*

Today I feel:

*One thing I love about myself is:*_____

Have you put a dream on hold because things didn't go as planned?
Do you regret your decision? It's never too late to chase after a dream.
How can you pick up where you left off?

_____

_____

_____

_____

_____

_____

_____

_____

_____

_____

_____

_____

_____

_____

_____

_____

Today I feel:

*One thing I love about myself is:*_____

Learning from our mistakes is the best way to improve our lives. Write down several mistakes you made, and what lesson you learned from each one.

_____

_____

_____

_____

_____

_____

_____

_____

_____

_____

_____

_____

_____

_____

"One of the lessons that I grew up with was to always stay true to yourself and never let what somebody else says distract you from your goals."

—MICHELLE OBAMA

Today I feel:

*One thing I love about myself is:*_____

When we are confident in ourselves, we have the power to achieve anything we desire. Building confidence requires us to work on ourselves. What is an area of your life that you would like to improve? What are some steps you can take to do so?

_____

_____

_____

_____

_____

_____

_____

_____

_____

_____

_____

_____

_____

_____

_____

Today I feel:

*One thing I love about myself is:*_____

You are talented and resourceful. Reflect on a time when your talent and resourcefulness helped you get closer to achieving your goals.

_____

_____

_____

_____

_____

_____

_____

_____

_____

_____

_____

_____

_____

_____

_____

_____

_____

EMMA GONZALEZ

Gun control activist Emma Gonzalez is an extraordinary example of the power of resilience. In February 2018, at 19 years old, Emma survived one of the deadliest high school shooting in American history, which took the lives of 17 people at Marjory Stoneman Douglas High School in Parkland, Florida.

In the wake of this tragedy, Emma decided to take action and cofounded Never Again MSD, a student-led gun control advocacy group. In an effort to raise awareness during the 2018 midterm elections, the group organized a bus tour to help register young people to vote. It was during this tour that Emma gave a speech against gun violence that went viral. The group went on to help organize March for Our Lives, one of the biggest youth-led protests in American history, attended by more than 200,000 people.

Emma Gonzalez was named one of *Time* magazine's 100 Most Influential People in 2018 and continues to make strides for the American public as an advocate for gun control.

Today I feel:

One thing I love about myself is:_____

When you believe you can achieve anything, nothing can stand in your way. Today, write down 10 reasons why nothing can stand in your way.

1. _____

2. _____

3. _____

4. _____

5. _____

6. _____

7. _____

8. _____

9. _____

10. _____

Today I feel:

One thing I love about myself is: _____

Who is your resilience icon? What obstacles did they have to overcome and how did they do so? What can you learn from their journey?

_____

_____

_____

_____

_____

_____

_____

_____

_____

_____

_____

_____

_____

_____

_____

_____

_____

Today I feel:

One thing I love about myself is:_____

When was the last time that you doubted yourself? Were those doubts rooted in truth or fear? Write a letter to your future self about the importance of letting go of self-doubt.

_____

_____

_____

_____

_____

_____

_____

_____

_____

_____

_____

_____

_____

_____

_____

"Only I can change my life. No one can do it for me."

—CAROL BURNETT

I Am Unique

Want to know one of the things that makes our planet such a beautiful place? We share it with more than seven billion people, but no two people are the same. Human nature designed each of us to be unique, but consumer culture and social media make it easy to feel like we are not enough.

How do we stop comparing ourselves to others? We have to recognize when this is happening and rise above it. You don't need to look like anyone else or have what anyone else has to feel confident in your own skin because you are a limited-edition model. There is nobody else in the world like you! Understanding this is the foundation to embracing your individuality and living your best life.

Today I feel:

*I am unique because:*_____

Set a timer for one minute. See how many things you can write down that you love about yourself during this time. When you're finished, circle the things that make you feel unique.

_____

_____

_____

_____

_____

_____

_____

_____

_____

_____

_____

_____

_____

_____

_____

_____

Today I feel:

I am unique because: _____

How do you currently express your individuality? Is it through fashion, schoolwork, or extracurricular activities? Are there other ways you desire to express your individuality?

_____

_____

_____

_____

_____

_____

_____

_____

_____

_____

_____

_____

_____

_____

_____

_____

_____

_____

Today I feel:

*I am unique because:*_____

Sometimes we get so caught up in the expectations of others that we forget to develop our own. What are your expectations for your life? What standards would you like to set for yourself?

_____

_____

_____

_____

_____

_____

_____

_____

_____

_____

_____

_____

_____

_____

_____

Today I feel:

*I am unique because:*_____

We risk losing our individuality when we view ourselves in a negative light. What negative thoughts around self-image do you need to eliminate? What steps can you take to get rid of them?

_____

_____

_____

_____

_____

_____

_____

_____

_____

_____

_____

_____

_____

_____

_____

_____

_____

Today I feel:

*I am unique because:*_____

Social media makes it so easy for us to compare ourselves with others, but negative comparison (as it's said) is almost always the thief of joy. Take a moment to consider the things that set you apart from your peers. How can these differences help you get ahead in life?

_____

_____

_____

_____

_____

_____

_____

_____

_____

_____

_____

_____

_____

_____

_____

_____

_____

"We need to reshape our own perception of how we view ourselves. We have to step up as women and take the lead."

—BEYONCÉ

Today I feel:

*I am unique because:*_____

What is your most unique quality? How do you plan to cultivate it as you grow older?

For example: *"I am really good at public speaking. As I grow older, I can seek out more opportunities that can help me hone this skill, like signing up for acting classes, joining the debate team, or creating my own YouTube channel."*

_____

_____

_____

_____

_____

_____

_____

_____

_____

_____

_____

_____

_____

_____

_____

LIZZO

There are many reasons why Lizzo has risen to superstardom over the last few years. She is a talented musician with a voice that is out of this world and a talent for playing the flute. She displays an incredible work ethic and is forthcoming about her struggles, which makes her relatable to her fan base—but there's something more to her.

She loves herself unconditionally while operating within an industry that is notorious for promoting a standard of beauty that looks nothing like her. She has become a body-positive icon for anyone who has ever struggled with embracing qualities that make them unique. Her music and performances ooze unconditional self-love, which might be why she was nominated for eight Grammy awards in 2020. That's more nominations than any other artist received that year.

If you ever need some self-love inspiration, Lizzo's music will put you in the right frame of mind.

Today I feel:

I am unique because: _____

Your friend just told you that a quality about herself makes her feel unhappy. Write two letters to her. One letter should be your response to her if this quality is one she cannot change and has to accept. The second letter should be your response to her if this quality is one that she can change.

_____

_____

_____

_____

_____

_____

_____

_____

_____

_____

_____

_____

_____

_____

_____

_____

Today I feel:

*I am unique because:*_____

Think about a time when standing out from the crowd impacted you in a positive way. How did that moment make you feel? How can you create more opportunities to embrace your individuality?

_____

_____

_____

_____

_____

_____

_____

_____

_____

_____

_____

_____

_____

_____

_____

LOVE YOURSELF

You have so much to be grateful for. Today, I'd like you to take a moment to think about what you appreciate about yourself and engage in an act of self-love. You could take a walk in your favorite park, give yourself a manicure, do your favorite exercise, or go outside and pick some flowers for your room.

Today I feel:

I am unique because: _____

Our individuality is not exclusive to our physical traits. What unique life experiences have shaped who you are as a person? How can you cultivate more unique experiences in the future?

_____

_____

_____

_____

_____

_____

_____

_____

_____

_____

_____

_____

_____

_____

Today I feel:

*I am unique because:*_____

Where do you see yourself in the next 5 to 10 years? How will your individuality play a role in getting you there?

_____

_____

_____

_____

_____

_____

_____

_____

_____

_____

_____

_____

_____

_____

_____

_____

_____

_____

Today I feel:

*I am unique because:*_____

We all have unique upbringings, viewpoints, and desires, and yet societal norms can try to change us. Take a moment to release all external expectations. They no longer exist. Now consider: What is your purpose? What do you desire out of life? What drives you as an individual?

_____

_____

_____

_____

_____

_____

_____

_____

_____

_____

_____

_____

_____

_____

_____

_____

_____

Today I feel:

I am unique because: _____

Self-acceptance is essential to leading a confident life. Do you have difficulty accepting certain things about yourself? What are those things? Are they things you can change? If so, how do you plan to work on that change? If they aren't things you can change, how can you work on accepting them?

_____

_____

_____

_____

_____

_____

_____

_____

_____

_____

_____

_____

_____

_____

_____

_____

MICHELLE OBAMA

We know her as the first African American First Lady of the United States of America, but Michelle Obama is so much more than that. She is an esteemed lawyer, author, and advocate for women and families.

Born in Chicago, Illinois, Michelle's parents nurtured her unique gift for cultivating her intelligence. She consistently performed at the highest academic level throughout her youth and went on to graduate *cum laude* from Princeton University before earning her law degree from Harvard Law School.

Her confidence and continual growth has garnered national attention since the 2004 Democratic National Convention. Michelle was essential to Barack Obama's campaign for president and made history by becoming the first African American First Lady of the United States.

Now, she is adored as a national icon of grace for her consistently refined responses to public scrutiny and racism on the world stage. She remains true to herself and continues to inspire many through her unique story.

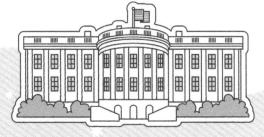

Today I feel:

I am unique because: _____

Life is a gift that we often take for granted. Gratitude is an important part of growth. What do you appreciate about where you are right now in your life? What do you love about your life?

_____

_____

_____

_____

_____

_____

_____

_____

_____

_____

_____

_____

_____

_____

_____

Today I feel:

*I am unique because:*_____

Are you different from your friends, family, and the people in your community? Good! You should be proud of the things that make you different, even in moments when it might feel hard. What differentiating characteristic are you most proud of?

_____

_____

_____

_____

_____

_____

_____

_____

_____

_____

_____

_____

_____

_____

Today I feel:

I am unique because: _____

Sometimes it can feel like we are living to please everyone but ourselves. What pleases you? What kinds of activities and experiences excite you?

_____

_____

_____

_____

_____

_____

_____

_____

_____

_____

_____

_____

_____

_____

"*Justice is about making sure that being polite is not the same thing as being quiet. In fact, often times, the most righteous thing you can do is shake the table.*"

—ALEXANDRIA OCASIO-CORTEZ

Today I feel:

*I am unique because:*_____

Have you ever questioned something mainstream, but felt too afraid to explore the thought? What was the thing you questioned? It's okay to question the status quo. It's part of how we evolve.

_____

_____

_____

_____

_____

_____

_____

_____

_____

_____

_____

_____

_____

_____

_____

Today I feel:

I am unique because: _____

There is no one way to approach life. You have options. In a perfect world, what would your life goals be? What would a week in your life look like?

_____

_____

_____

_____

_____

_____

_____

_____

_____

_____

_____

_____

_____

_____

_____

_____

Today I feel:

*I am unique because:*_____

Oftentimes we sacrifice our own desires in order to please others. This is dangerous because when we live for the approval of others, we deprioritize the most important opinion of all—our own. This can threaten the elements of our personality that make us unique, and that's not what we want at all. Are there any elements of your life that you are not pleased with? What are they and how can you change them?

_____

_____

_____

_____

_____

_____

_____

_____

_____

_____

_____

_____

SELF-IDENTITY DANCE

Let's practice embracing our individuality through dance. First, think of a song that celebrates self-love. Here are a few examples to get you started: "Level Up" by Ciara, "Flawless" by Beyonce, and "Roar" by Katy Perry. Now, I want you to play that song in a private space, or maybe on your headphones, and start dancing. Block out all of the negative thoughts in your head and just dance like no one is watching—because nobody is! This is your time to embrace yourself.

Today I feel:

*I am unique because:*_____

Limiting beliefs are internal thoughts that consciously and unconsciously hold us back. What limiting beliefs do you have around your individuality? Consider why these limiting beliefs are untrue. What tactics can you implement to work past them so that you can live your best life?

_____

_____

_____

_____

_____

_____

_____

_____

_____

_____

_____

_____

_____

_____

_____

_____

_____

_____

Today I feel:

*I am unique because:*_____

What daily practices can you implement to get you closer to embracing your individuality? Come up with a detailed plan to execute this practice. What time of day will this practice take place? Is it something that you can do no matter where you are? Be realistic.

For example: *A daily practice that I can implement to get closer to embracing my individuality is asking myself what I desire out of my day, and then planning how I can achieve those goals before getting my day started.*

MONDAY_____

_____

TUESDAY_____

_____

WEDNESDAY_____

_____

THURSDAY_____

_____

FRIDAY_____

_____

SATURDAY_____

_____

SUNDAY_____

"*I say if I'm beautiful. I say if I'm strong. You will not determine my story—I will.*"

—AMY SCHUMER

Today I feel:

*I am unique because:*_____

Think about your upbringing. What about your family, neighborhood, and childhood friendships stands out as unique? How has this shaped you as a person?

_____

_____

_____

_____

_____

_____

_____

_____

_____

_____

_____

_____

_____

_____

_____

Today I feel:

I am unique because: _____

Sometimes we have to let go of our thoughts to learn how to embrace ourselves more. Things like yoga, meditation, dancing, and hiking are awesome ways to let go of external pressure and feel more connected to ourselves. Think about something introspective that you would like to try. What do you hope it will help you let go of? How will it make you feel? How will you get started?

_____

_____

_____

_____

_____

_____

_____

_____

_____

_____

_____

_____

_____

LADY GAGA

Nobody reinvents themselves more than Lady Gaga. This native New Yorker learned how to march to the beat of her own drum early in life and it has served her extremely well. She discovered her passion for music at the age of 4 and began performing in New York City nightclubs at 14. She became one of only 20 students across the globe to be granted early acceptance into New York University's Tisch School of the Arts, where she studied music and songwriting for a few years before withdrawing to find her own way of doing things. Talk about taking the road less traveled!

Lady Gaga spent years performing in nightclubs and working as a songwriter until her own career took off. She became an international pop sensation known for her eclectic fashion, empowering music, and vibrant performance style. In fact, she received a lot of criticism for embracing these unique qualities about herself, but she never let that stop her from shining her light. Instead, she continues to remain true to herself and encourages others to do the same through her creative endeavors and extensive anti-bullying, LBGTQ+ rights, and mental health awareness activism.

Today I feel:

*I am unique because:*_____

Have you ever been the first to do or try something in your family or friend group? If not, do you want to be? How does this make you unique?

_____

_____

_____

_____

_____

_____

_____

_____

_____

_____

_____

_____

_____

_____

Today I feel:

*I am unique because:*_____

Complete the following phrases and write down ways that you can cultivate environments to support your individuality:

- *I feel unique when:*_____

  _____

  _____

  _____

- *I am proud of my differences when:*_____

  _____

  _____

  _____

- *I try new things when:*_____

  _____

  _____

  _____

Today I feel:

I am unique because: _____

You are magically 10 years older. Write a letter to your younger self explaining how learning to embrace your uniqueness had a positive impact on your life.

_____

_____

_____

_____

_____

_____

_____

_____

_____

_____

_____

_____

_____

_____

_____

_____

I Am Brave

Bravery is a quality that lives within us all, so how do we harness it? We do so by taking time to explore our feelings, wishes, desires, and fears. Brave women are honest with themselves and they practice acknowledging their truth no matter how easy or difficult the situation is.

Bravery is about tapping into your inner strength to grow as an individual and lead by example. It is important to understand that bravery can show up in many ways. It can be loud, but it can also be quiet. It can mean taking a stand or refusing to stand.

There is no single way to demonstrate bravery. It's about letting go of fear and embracing what you know to be true deep down inside.

Today I feel:

Today I will be brave by: _____

What does bravery mean to you?

_____

_____

_____

_____

_____

_____

_____

_____

_____

_____

_____

_____

_____

_____

_____

_____

_____

Today I feel:

*Today I will be brave by:*_____

Bravery can feel hard or easy based on the circumstance of each situation. At what times do you find it easy to be brave? At what times do you find it hard to be brave?

_____

_____

_____

_____

_____

_____

_____

_____

_____

_____

_____

_____

_____

_____

_____

_____

_____

Today I feel:

Today I will be brave by: _____

A non-negotiable personal value is something that you cherish about yourself and are committed to preserving no matter what. What are your non-negotiable personal values? How do you plan to preserve them when they are threatened?

For example: *My non-negotiable personal value is being proud of who I am no matter what. Sometimes, in group settings, it can be easy to fall into the trap of comparing myself with others, but in those moments, I will choose to think of all of the positive qualities that I have instead of focusing on what I lack.*

_____

_____

_____

_____

_____

_____

_____

_____

_____

_____

_____

_____

Today I feel:

*Today I will be brave by:*_____

When was the last time that you were brave? How did it make
you feel?

_____

_____

_____

_____

_____

_____

_____

_____

_____

_____

_____

_____

_____

_____

_____

_____

_____

_____

Today I feel:

Today I will be brave by: _____

Bravery often requires us to be honest about our desires. Have you ever downplayed what you truly wanted? Why? And how can you commit to changing that in the future?

_____

_____

_____

_____

_____

_____

_____

_____

_____

_____

_____

_____

_____

_____

> "You get in life what you have the courage to ask for."
>
> —OPRAH WINFREY

Today I feel:

Today I will be brave by:_____

How do you show up for yourself every day? Do you align your behavior with your desires? Share examples of how you can channel bravery in your day-to-day life.

_____

_____

_____

_____

_____

_____

_____

_____

_____

_____

_____

_____

_____

_____

HARRIET TUBMAN

Harriet Tubman is one of the bravest women in American history. Her incredible story began in the early 1800s when she was born into slavery in Maryland. As an enslaved person, she was subjected to countless beatings and injuries at the hands of her enslavers.

By 1849, she decided to risk her life and attempt to escape from slavery by traveling to the North. Her effort was a dangerous one, but proved to be successful as she made it to the North safely. Her brave decision would be the first of many as she decided to return to the South more than 19 times to free over 300 enslaved people.

She went on to serve as a scout and nurse for the Union forces during the Civil War, and even spied on the Confederates for the 2nd South Carolina Volunteer Infantry Regiment. Harriet's contributions to ending slavery were incredible and her legacy will continue to live on. The White House is currently working on placing her image on the $20 bill.

Today I feel:

Today I will be brave by: _____

What do you want out of life this week? How can you be bold about your desires? Who can you ask for help? Knowing when to ask for help is a sign of self-awareness, strength, and bravery. Write down your plan for attaining everything you want out of this week.

_____

_____

_____

_____

_____

_____

_____

_____

_____

_____

_____

_____

_____

_____

Today I feel:

Today I will be brave by: _____

What does inner strength mean to you?

_____

_____

_____

_____

_____

_____

_____

_____

_____

_____

_____

_____

_____

_____

_____

_____

_____

_____

_____

VISUALIZING BRAVERY

Close your eyes and visualize your bravest self. As you visualize this version of yourself, consider what you look like, how you feel, the way that you think, and how you live your life. Imagine a day in the life of your bravest self. Feel free to draw your bravest self, or make mental notes in the blank space below.

Today I feel:

*Today I will be brave by:*_____

Let's expand the vision of your bravest self. Who is she friends with? What are her daily habits? How does she show up for herself?

_____

_____

_____

_____

_____

_____

_____

_____

_____

_____

_____

_____

_____

_____

_____

_____

_____

Today I feel:

*Today I will be brave by:*_____

Bravery requires us to be honest with ourselves. In today's entry, stretch yourself to be truly honest and answer these questions for yourself: What is your truth? What is your purpose?

_____

_____

_____

_____

_____

_____

_____

_____

_____

_____

_____

_____

_____

> "No one can make you feel inferior without your consent."
>
> —ELEANOR ROOSEVELT

Today I feel:

Today I will be brave by: _____

Trust is the foundation of living fearlessly. What will it take for you to trust yourself enough to stand firm in your values?

_____

_____

_____

_____

_____

_____

_____

_____

_____

_____

_____

_____

_____

_____

_____

_____

_____

_____

Today I feel:

*Today I will be brave by:*_____

Confidence in any area of our lives can be gained by doing something repeatedly. Think about your daily routine. How can you practice being bolder in your day-to-day life?

_____

_____

_____

_____

_____

_____

_____

_____

_____

_____

_____

_____

_____

_____

_____

AMELIA EARHART

American aviator Amelia Earhart took bravery to new heights. The Kansas native experienced her first airplane ride at the age of 23 and the rest was history. A year later, she purchased her first plane and began taking flying lessons.

In 1932, she became the first female aviator to fly solo across the Atlantic Ocean, and she did so in record time, despite a few mechanical difficulties. It was the first of many incredible achievements. She continued to fly throughout the world, wrote three books, served as an aviation editor for *Cosmopolitan* magazine, and founded an international organization for women pilots before her untimely disappearance in 1937.

Today I feel:

Today I will be brave by: _____

Bravery starts from within and radiates out into the world. What fears are taking up space in your mind? Instead of viewing these fears as obstacles to hold you back, consider how you can approach them as opportunities to explore new things in a brave way.

_____

_____

_____

_____

_____

_____

_____

_____

_____

_____

_____

_____

_____

_____

_____

_____

Today I feel:

*Today I will be brave by:*_____

Bravery can often feel intimidating and isolating because it is associated with standing out from the crowd. However, bravery doesn't always show up in that way. Consider different styles of bravery that you witness from friends or family. Bravery can come from choosing a unique path, standing up for others, quietly taking a stand, and removing yourself from situations you disagree with—among many other examples. What kind of bravery most aligns with you as a person?

_____

_____

_____

_____

_____

_____

_____

_____

_____

_____

_____

Today I feel:

*Today I will be brave by:*_____

Who is the bravest person you know? What do you like about their personal style of bravery?

_____

_____

_____

_____

_____

_____

_____

_____

_____

_____

_____

_____

_____

_____

_____

_____

_____

_____

_____

"Take chances, make mistakes.
That's how you grow.
Pain nourishes your courage.
You have to fail in order to
practice being brave."

—MARY TYLER MOORE

Today I feel:

*Today I will be brave by:*_____

Bravery requires inner work. What areas in your life require improvement? Are you working toward healing from things in your past or present? Consider how you can start to work on becoming the best version of yourself. This can mean seeking out a mentor, support group, or tutor. The sky is the limit.

_____

_____

_____

_____

_____

_____

_____

_____

_____

_____

_____

_____

_____

_____

_____

Today I feel:

*Today I will be brave by:*_____

You have so many amazing qualities. What are they and how can they influence others to be brave?

_____

_____

_____

_____

_____

_____

_____

_____

_____

_____

_____

_____

_____

_____

_____

_____

Today I feel:

*Today I will be brave by:*_____

Consider a time when you wanted to be brave but couldn't be. How did it make you feel? In hindsight, what choices could you have made to be brave in that moment?

_____

_____

_____

_____

_____

_____

_____

_____

_____

_____

_____

_____

_____

_____

BRAVERY SPEECH

Stand in front of the mirror and practice giving a speech to your friends on bravery. What are the benefits of staying true to yourself and being brave? How can being brave elevate your friend group for the better? How will this make you all better in the long run?

Today I feel:

*Today I will be brave by:*_____

We are all born with characteristics that make us unique and power-ful. What makes me powerful will be different from what makes you powerful and that's okay. What are five characteristics that make you powerful?

For example: *"I am powerful because I am really good at learning from my mistakes."*

1. _____
   _____
   _____

2. _____
   _____
   _____

3. _____
   _____
   _____

4. _____
   _____

5. _____
   _____

Today I feel:

Today I will be brave by: _____

Sometimes we can have fears that are so great we try to ignore them instead of identifying them. However, the sooner we understand our fears, the easier it will be for us to face them and live in our truth. What are your greatest fears, and how do you plan to push past them in life?

_____

_____

_____

_____

_____

_____

_____

_____

_____

_____

_____

_____

_____

_____

"'Brave' is very specific and extremely personal. It can't be judged by people on the outside. Just can't. Sometimes brave means letting everyone else think you're a coward. Sometimes brave is letting everyone else down but yourself."

—GLENNON DOYLE

Today I feel:

*Today I will be brave by:*_____

What risks would you like to take in life and why haven't you taken them yet? What would help you feel comfortable with taking these risks?

_____

_____

_____

_____

_____

_____

_____

_____

_____

_____

_____

_____

_____

_____

Today I feel:

*Today I will be brave by:*_____

The people that we surround ourselves with have a huge impact on the way we live our lives. Consider your friend group. What are the qualities that you like about your friends? What are the qualities that you dislike about your friends? Do the good qualities outweigh the less-desirable qualities? How does this make you feel?

_____

_____

_____

_____

_____

_____

_____

_____

_____

_____

_____

_____

_____

_____

ROSA PARKS

Civil rights activist Rosa Parks's bravery was so powerful that it set a series of iconic events in motion that ultimately changed the fabric of American society.

During the height of segregation in the South, Rosa Parks was instructed to give up her seat on a bus to a white passenger. When she refused, she was arrested and taken to jail. Her bravery served as the catalyst to the Montgomery Bus Boycott, an iconic movement in which the African American community refused to take public transportation for more than a year. The boycott ended with a Supreme Court ruling that deemed segregation on buses as unconstitutional.

Despite experiencing retaliation in the form of losing her job and receiving death threats, Rosa Parks became an international civil rights icon and worked alongside notable civil rights leaders like Martin Luther King, Jr., to help legally end segregation in America.

Today I feel:

*Today I will be brave by:*_____

What is the bravest thing that you've ever done? What about that moment makes you most proud?

_____

_____

_____

_____

_____

_____

_____

_____

_____

_____

_____

_____

_____

_____

_____

_____

_____

_____

_____

_____

Today I feel:

Today I will be brave by: _____

Sometimes being brave is as simple as accepting the things that make us unique in a world in which everyone strives to be the same. Would you agree or disagree with the statement? Why or why not?

_____

_____

_____

_____

_____

_____

_____

_____

_____

_____

_____

_____

_____

_____

_____

Today I feel:

Today I will be brave by: _____

Have you ever regretted not going after something you wanted because of fear? Explore that regret and consider how you can avoid regret in the future by channeling bravery.

_____

_____

_____

_____

_____

_____

_____

_____

_____

_____

_____

_____

_____

_____

_____

_____

"When you feel powerful, you are willing to stand up for your rights, you are willing to stand up for what you believe in, you're more willing to stand up and be counted."

—MARGARET CHO

RESOURCES

Because I Was a Girl: True Stories for Girls of All Ages by Melissa de la Cruz

Becoming by Michelle Obama

Bossypants by Tina Fey

Is Everyone Hanging Out Without Me? by Mindy Kaling

More Than Enough: Claiming Space for Who You Are by Elaine Welteroth

Teen Trailblazers: 30 Fearless Girls Who Changed the World Before They Were 20 by Jennifer Calvert

The Power of Positive Thinking by Dr. Norman Vincent Peale

Year of Yes by Shonda Rhimes

About the Author

Charmaine Charmant is a New York City native of Caribbean descent with a passion for women's empowerment and fashion. She earned her BA from Wellesley College and her MS in Management from Wake Forest University prior to becoming a fashion and lifestyle content creator. Her work, which encourages women to embrace their individuality and live confidently in style, has been featured on ABC 7, xoNecole, and Buzzfeed. To learn more about Charmaine, you can visit her website CharmaineCharmant.com.

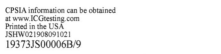
CPSIA information can be obtained
at www.ICGtesting.com
Printed in the USA
JSHW021908091021
19373JS00006B/9